The Luminous Landscape

*Zhang Lu (active ca. 1500): "Monk."
Hanging scroll, ink on silk (69 x 35 1/2
inches). Courtesy of the Royal Ontario
Museum, Toronto, Canada.*

The Luminous Landscape

CHINESE ART AND POETRY

Edited by Richard Lewis

DOUBLEDAY & COMPANY, INC., GARDEN CITY, NEW YORK

Library of Congress Catalog Card Number 79–7691
ISBN: 0-385-14712-0 Trade
ISBN: 0-385-14713-9 Prebound

Calligraphy by Loretta Pan

The romanization used in this book, pin-yin, is the official system
that has been adopted by the People's Republic of China.

In memory of Gandy Brodie,
who, in his art, also sought the luminous.

Also edited by Richard Lewis

IN PRAISE OF MUSIC
THE MOMENT OF WONDER
IN A SPRING GARDEN
MIRACLES
MOON, FOR WHAT DO YOU WAIT?
THE WIND AND THE RAIN
OUT OF THE EARTH I SING
THE PARK
OF THIS WORLD
JOURNEYS
MUSE OF THE ROUND SKY
STILL WATERS OF THE AIR
THE WAY OF SILENCE
THERE ARE TWO LIVES
I BREATHE A NEW SONG

Hua Yan (1682–1758): "Two Mynah Birds on a Branch: A Squirrel Leaping for a Wild Grape Vine." (23 3/4 x 52 7/8 inches). Courtesy of the Smithsonian Institution, Freer Gallery of Art, Washington, D.C.

Introduction

On a gravestone in China there is an epitaph to the Chinese painter Yuan Meng-hui:

> In the mountains
> One sees
> Human-heartedness
> In water, wisdom.

Here, in brief, was the essence of a view of life and nature that speaks to us today with renewed poignancy. It is an insight which emerged from a brilliant civilization concerned with probing and expressing the profound relationship between the human experience of nature and nature itself. The very laws of that civilization, in part, were governed by their understanding of this experience—and subsequently that civilization produced some of the most extraordinary works of art and poetry known to the world.

The basis of this civilization, Dao,* was a belief that all of nature, whether it be mountains, rocks, streams, or trees, was indeed *alive*. Each element had an individuality that spoke of something more than just what it was on the surface—each had qualities which were characteristic of the principles of life. A rock was not simply a rock and a mountain was not simply a mountain: They were vibrant with what the Chinese called "qi"† or spirit. For the poet and painter of China, the challenge and inspiration was to capture this spirit—to dive down into the very center of these things in order to reveal the power and pulsation of nature as it manifested itself in themselves and the things around

* or Tao, as it is more commonly known in the old romanization.
† or "ch'i," as it is more commonly known in the old romanization.

them. The task of the poet and the painter then was to become so familiar with the objects of nature that they could express the dual nature of themselves and the elements of nature as one. As a Chinese poet said: "Heaven and Earth live together, and all things and I are one."

To look at a flower, a bird, or a mountain was more than just looking —it was a way of seeing beyond their initial qualities into the "heart" of these things. The painter Fan Kuan spent months wandering through the snow observing mountains in order to paint the "very bones of the mountains." The poet Ruan Ji begins one of his poems by saying:

> "Inscribe on your heart,
>   Every inch of time at sunset."

Art and poetry in China were closely allied. This was due in part to the role of calligraphy, in which the actual writing of words was based on depicting an image or representation of the word itself. Thus a tree in calligraphy is 木 , a mountain is 山 , the moon is 月 , the rain is 雨 , etc. Very often poets and painters collaborated. In many instances poems were actually inscribed on the paintings themselves. Perhaps the old Chinese proverb "A picture is a voiceless poem, a poem is a vocal picture" best summarizes the intermingling of these two art forms.

The intent of this book is not to present a scholarly or historical overview of Chinese painting and poetry, but to present examples of works concerned with evoking the particular world of Chinese landscape. One might ask, "What relevance does such a world have for us today? Why should one go back to an artistic tradition that had its beginnings nearly three thousand years ago in order to bring oneself closer to an understanding of the nature of landscape?" These questions can be answered in a number of ways. First, as our own culture becomes increasingly threatened by the destruction of its natural environment, there is no better example of the role which the natural world can play in the spiritual health of a country than that which existed in China. Second, the expression in painting and poetry of this wonderfully balanced relationship between man and his environment is one of the high points of artistic achievement to be found in any culture. Certainly the marriage and interdependence of two art forms such as poetry and painting have rarely occurred with such purity and refinement. It is also possible for them to act as a stimulus for us to approach the very "heart" of nature with a renewed appreciation.

Like the Chinese poets and painters, we are capable of going beyond the mere surface of our experience of nature—into the deeper pulse of the "aliveness" of things. We too can travel along the paths taken by persons whose lives can still be heard through their creations, because these creations, like the nature they so admired and respected, were a part of the life they lived. Poetry and painting were not mere activities designed to entertain, they were truths passed from one person to another for generations. They were ways of transmitting the elements of life through forms that were understood to be ways of life.

Because in Chinese the term for landscape painting is "shan-shui" or "mountain-water picture," I have divided this book into two sections— Waters and Mountains. The works chosen for each section were not originally written or painted for each other, but I have chosen to bring them together as illuminations of similar themes and feelings. At various points in the book I have also inserted prose statements by critics, poets, and painters who have written on the art of landscape painting.

My hope is that this book will be similar to the experience that Xie He spoke of when he said: "The silence of a thousand years seems to be broken as one unrolls these paintings and gazes upon them." I hope, as well, that once such a silence has been broken, we might be able to participate again in a landscape luminous with the vitality of its own life— and suggestive, in every way, of our necessary dependence on that life.

RL

Waters

. . . is not water, whether trickling, flowing, spraying, foaming, splashing, or in rivers or oceans, the very blood and marrow of Heaven and Earth? Blood nourishes the bones. Bones without marrow are dead bones. Such bones are like dry soil and can no longer be called bones. Mountains are bones, since water has formed them, and for this reason the ancients paid careful attention to painting waterfalls.

Jie Zi Yuan Hua Zhuan

West Lake

One day I walk by the lake.
One day I sit by the lake.
One day I stand by the lake.
One day I lie by the lake.

Yuan Hong-dao

Thoughts While Reading

The mirror of the pond gleams,
Half an acre in size.
The splendor of the sky,
And the whiteness of the clouds
Are reflected back upon themselves.
I ask the pond where I can find
Anything else as pure and transparent.
"Only in the springs of the water of life."

Zhu Xi

Qian Du (1763–1844): "Record of the Bamboo Hall at Huang Kang." Album leaf mounted as hanging scroll, ink and color on paper (9 1/4 x 10 1/2 inches). Courtesy of the Royal Ontario Museum, Toronto, Canada.

14

Fisherman

The wind blows the line out from his fishing pole.
In a straw hat and grass cape the fisherman
Is invisible in the long reeds.
In the fine spring rain it is impossible to see very far
And the mist rising from the water has hidden the hills.

Ouyang Xiu

Miscellaneous Poem at Three Lakes

Distant water
　　spread out behind misty trees
with a few black dots
　　among the waves:
it is like a newly finished painting,
the rich ink still slightly moist.

Yuan Zhong-dao

Fisher Folk on the River

Men who come and go on the river,
All enjoy the savor of perch.
Pray look at that leaf-like boat,
Now seen, now unseen, in the windy waves.

                            Fan Zhong-yan

Li Song (active ca. 1190–1230): "The Red Cliff." Ink and slight color on silk (10 x 10 2/5 inches). (Nelson Fund), Nelson Gallery-Atkins Museum, Kansas City.

18

Distant men have no eyes; distant trees have no
branches. Distant mountains have no stones, and they
are as fine and delicate as eyebrows. Distant water
has no ripples, and reaches up to the clouds. These
are the secrets.

Wang Wei

Duckweed Pond

Broad and deep lies the pond in spring.
I wait to meet the light skiff returning;
Green duckweed closes in the wake of the boat—
Then the weeping willow brushes it wide apart
once more.

Wang Wei

Style of Xia Gui (1180–1230): "River Landscape with Boatman." Album leaf, ink on silk (9 1/8 x 9 1/2 inches). The Metropolitan Museum of Art, New York, Fletcher Fund, 1947.

At the Rapids of the Luan Family

Under the spatter of October rain
The shallow water slides over slippery stones;
Leaping waves strike each other
And frightened, the egret dares not dive for fish.

Wang Wei

Large and small rocks mingle and are related like the pieces on a chessboard. Small rocks near water are like children gathered around with arms outstretched toward the mother rock. On a mountain it is the large rock, the elder, that seems to reach out and gather the children about him. There is kinship among rocks.

Jie Zi Yuan Hua Zhuan

Egret Dyke

Swoop! The egret dives into the red lotus blossoms.
Splash! He breaks the clear water into waves.
How handsome he looks in his new-born feathered silk
Proudly balanced on the old raft, a fish in his beak . . .

Wang Wei

Unidentified artist: "Crane." Hanging scroll, ink and slight color on silk (74 1/4 x 37 1/2 inches). The Metropolitan Museum of Art, New York, Anonymous Gift, 1948.

Written While Viewing the River in Autumn

Egrets asleep on the vast sand-drift,
A strip of water, not a blemish
Soaking the blue sky.
I love most the reed flowers just after the rains.
A sail and smoke;
They are cooking food in the fishing boat.

Lin Bu

Dai Jin (1388–1462): "Fishermen on the River" (detail). Ink and color on paper (18 1/8 x 291 3/8 inches). Courtesy of the Smithsonian Institution, Freer Gallery of Art, Washington, D.C.

*Mu Xi (active 1736–96): "Eight Views of Hsiao Hsiang."
Album leaf, ink and color on paper (20 3/4 x 25 inches).
Courtesy of the Royal Ontario Museum, Toronto,
Canada.*

Lotus Pool

Unafraid of the dashing rain on the pool,
Enameled leaves conceal each other.
Colorful birds suddenly fly in alarm,
Their rush scatters the sunset glow on the ripples.

Mei Yao-chen

Li Kan (1245–1320): "Ink–Bamboo." Ink on paper (14 3/4 x 93 1/2 inches).
(Nelson Fund), Nelson Gallery-Atkins Museum, Kansas City.

A Poem

High and lofty, tiers of rock,
How solitary it stands.
Luckily, in this strong wind the green bamboos cluster;
Sun sets, no one about, sea gulls have left.
Only the distant water remains,
Keeping company with the cold reeds.

Su Shi

In the Evening I Walk by the River

The frozen river is drifted deep with snow.
For days, only a few spots near the bank have
    stayed open.
In the evening when everyone has gone home,
The cormorants roost on the boats of the fishermen.

                  Ouyang Xiu

Artist unknown: "River Hamlet."
(Twelfth Century.) Fan-shaped album leaf,
ink and slight color on silk (9 1/2 x 10 inches).
Courtesy of the collection of
John M. Crawford, Jr., New York.

Gao Ke-ming: "Clearing After Snow on the River." (Dated 1035.) First section from a handscroll, ink and colors on silk (height 16 1/2 inches). Courtesy of the collection of John M. Crawford, Jr., New York.

The river is white in itself;
now brilliant snow fills sky and earth.
The river has a sound of its own;
now add the roar of a furious wind.

Yuan Zhong-dao

When the wind subsides, waves and ripples calm down.
When the clouds part, the moon emerges. The moonlit
mists are vast and boundless, and the eye cannot see
their limits. Rivers, seas, brooks, and ponds all in
one moment may suddenly become cold, calm, and silent.
Thus the nature of still waters may be revealed.

Jie Zi Yuan Hua Zhuan

*Gao Ke-ming: "Clearing After Snow on the River." (Dated 1035.) Final section
from a handscroll, ink and colors on silk (height 16 1/2 inches). Courtesy of the
collection of John M. Crawford, Jr., New York.*

Flowers and Moonlight on the Spring River

The evening river is level and motionless—
The spring colors just open to their full.
Suddenly a wave carries the moon away
And the tidal water comes with its freight of stars.

                              Yang-di

Night Rain at Guang-Kou

The river is clear and calm;
        a fast rain falls in the gorge.
At midnight the cold, splashing sound begins,
like thousands of pearls spilling onto a glass plate,
each drop penetrating the bone.

In my dream I scratch my head and get up to listen.
I listen and listen, until the dawn.
All my life I have heard rain,
        and I am an old man;
but now for the first time I understand
        the sound of spring rain
                on the river at night.

                              Yang Wan-li

Anonymous (Ming, Fifteenth Century): "Boat at Anchor by Reeds." Ink on silk (9 1/2 x 9 3/5 inches). Ross Collection 29.963. Courtesy, Museum of Fine Arts, Boston.

31

Mu Xi (active 1736–96): "Eight Views of Hsiao Hsiang."
Album leaf, ink and color on paper (20 3/ 4 x 25
inches). Courtesy of the Royal Ontario Museum,
Toronto, Canada.

When the moon is reflected on water, the waves are
like galloping white horses, and at that moment one
sees lofty mountains and peaks in their full grandeur.

Jie Zi Yuan Hua Zhuan

Morning Breaks over the Huai River

The pale moon drives the clouds towards the dawn;
A slight breeze blows across the water, ruffling the
    fishes' green scales.
Now I have decided to grow old with these rivers and
    lakes;
Silently I count ten waves coming from the middle of
    the Huai.

Su Shi

Among a thousand clouds and ten thousand streams,
Here lives an idle man,
In the daytime wandering over green mountains,
At night coming home to sleep by the cliff.
Swiftly the springs and autumns pass,
But my mind is at peace, free from dust or delusion.
How pleasant, to know I need nothing to lean on,
To be still as the waters of the autumn river!

Han-shan

Artist unknown (Thirteenth Century): Fan-shaped album leaf, ink and slight color on silk (10 7/8 x 10 5/8 inches). Courtesy of the collection of John M. Crawford, Jr., New York.

35

Style of Xia Gui (Sung, Twelfth and Thirteenth Centuries): "A Fisherman's Abode After Rain." Ink and color on silk (57 3/4 x 40 1/2 inches). Chinese and Japanese Special Fund 14.54. Courtesy, Museum of Fine Arts, Boston.

Mountains

. . . haze, mist, and the haunting spirits of the
mountains are what human nature seeks, and yet
can rarely find.

Guo Xi

On Sound

Ten thousand things are heard when born,
But the highest heaven's always still.
Yet everything must begin in silence.
And into silence it vanishes.

Wei Ying-wu

In the Mountains

I follow the moon into the mountains,
I search for clouds to accompany me home.
A spring morning, dew on the flowers:
and the fragrance clings to my gown.

Wang An-shi

*Shen Chuan (ca. 1682–1760): "Birds and Flowers—
Dragonfly on Wisteria." Ink on silk (10 1/2 x
8 inches). Coolidge Fund 67.717. Courtesy, Museum
of Fine Arts, Boston.*

Clouds on the Mountain

A shower passes across the blue sky,
Mountain clouds return to the tallest peaks.
Forest edge hides the rainbow,
Moving shadows descend the stream.
I return to see the parrots fly,
Once more I love this mountain peace.

Mei Yao-chen

Gong Xian (1617[8?]–89): "Mist-filled Valleys in the Manner of Mi Fei." One of ten album leaves mounted as scrolls, ink and slight color on paper (9 1/2 x 17 5/8 inches). (Nelson Fund), Nelson Gallery-Atkins Museum, Kansas City.

Deer Forest Hermitage

Through the deep wood, the slanting sunlight
Casts motley patterns on the jade-green mosses.
No glimpse of man in this lonely mountain,
Yet faint voices drift on the air.

Wang Wei

A Forest Lane Covered with Moss

Summer rain makes the forest muddy;
Slanting sunbeams reflect again and again.
Pure green, no wind ruffles it;
Let the spring grass smile!

Mei Yao-chen

摹范華原
秋山華意
梓煕

Mu Xi (active 1736–96): "Eight Views of Hsiao Hsiang."
Album leaf, ink and color on paper (20 3/4 x 25 inches).
Courtesy of the Royal Ontario Museum, Toronto,
Canada.

43

44

. . . there was one gigantic pine-tree; its aged
bark was overgrown with green lichen, and its
winged scales seemed to ride in the air. In
stature it was like that of the coiling dragon
which tries to reach the Milky Way.

Jing Hao

I climb the road to Cold Mountain,
The road to Cold Mountain that never ends.
The valleys are long and strewn with stones;
The streams broad and banked with thick grass.
The moss is slippery, though no rain has fallen;
Pines sigh, but it is not the wind.
Who can break from the snares of the world
And sit with me among the white clouds?

Han-shan

*Anonymous (Yuan Period): "Forest and Peaks of Tai-bai Mountain." Horizontal
scroll painting (11 1/2 x 109 4/5 inches). Keith McLeod Fund 55.618. Courtesy,
Museum of Fine Arts, Boston.*

Sitting Alone in Jing-ting Mountain

Flocks of birds fly high and vanish;
A single cloud, alone, calmly drifts on.
Never tired of looking at each other—
Only the Jing-ting Mountain and me.

Li Bo

Clouds are the ornaments of sky and earth, the
embroidery of mountains and streams. They may move
as swiftly as horses. They may seem to strike a
mountain with such force that one almost hears the
sound of the impact.

Jie Zi Yuan Hua Zhuan

*Mu Xi (active 1736–96): "Eight Views of Hsiao Hsiang." Album leaf, ink and color
on paper (20 3/4 x 25 inches). Courtesy of the Royal Ontario Museum,
Toronto, Canada.*

Inscribed on a Painting

White clouds, like a belt, wind around the waist of
    the mountains;
A path narrow and long soars into the void, off a
    stony ledge.
Alone, I lean on a thornwood staff and gaze peacefully
    into the distance;
Wishing to respond with my flute playing to the singing
    of the mountain stream.

Shen Zhou

Xu Dao-ning (died ca. 1066–67): "Fishermen." Handscroll in ink on silk (19 x 82 1/2 inches). (Nelson Fund), Nelson Gallery-Atkins Museum, Kansas City.

Distant Hills

Thousands of ridges stab at the clouds;
One glance is not enough.
Frontal ranges and the distant peaks,
Purplish blue, deep and light.

Mei Yao-chen

In the evening view, the mountains embrace the
crimson of the setting sun; sails are furled, and
boats are in the inlets. Men on the road are
hurrying on their way, and the brushwood gates of
the cottages are half-closed.

Wang Wei

Quatrain

Late sun, the stream and the hills; the beauty
Spring breeze, flowers and grasses; the fragrance
Steaming mudflat, swallows flying.
Warm sand, and mated ducks, asleep.

Du Fu

Looking at Yue-Tai Mountain from the Lian-Tian Pavilion

At sunset the green mountain is pale one moment,
   dark the next,
brushed by layers of floating mist.
Thousands of cloud scrolls enfold the peak
in a screen of red brocade.

Yang Wan-li

Attributed to Shen Sheng (c. 1465–87): "Hundred Geese." (9 x 89 1/5 inches).
Bequest of Charles Hoyt 50.1455. Courtesy, Museum of Fine Arts, Boston.

The Hill of the Hatchet-Leaved Bamboos

In the white moonlight the stream
    winds its way
    and disappears from sight.
The green of the bamboos
    grows denser,
    and then spills over.
Without pause
    I push on along the mountain road;
I walk and sing,
    my eyes on the familiar summits.

            Pei

The Hill of Hua-Tzŭ

The sun sets,
    the wind rises among the pines.
Returning home,
    there is a little dew upon the grass.
The reflection of the clouds
    falls into the tracks of my shoes,
The blue of the mountains
    touches my clothes.

            Pei

Attributed to Wu Wei (1459–1508): "Travellers." Hanging scroll, ink on coarse silk (61 1/2 x 38 1/2 inches). Courtesy of the Royal Ontario Museum, Toronto, Canada.

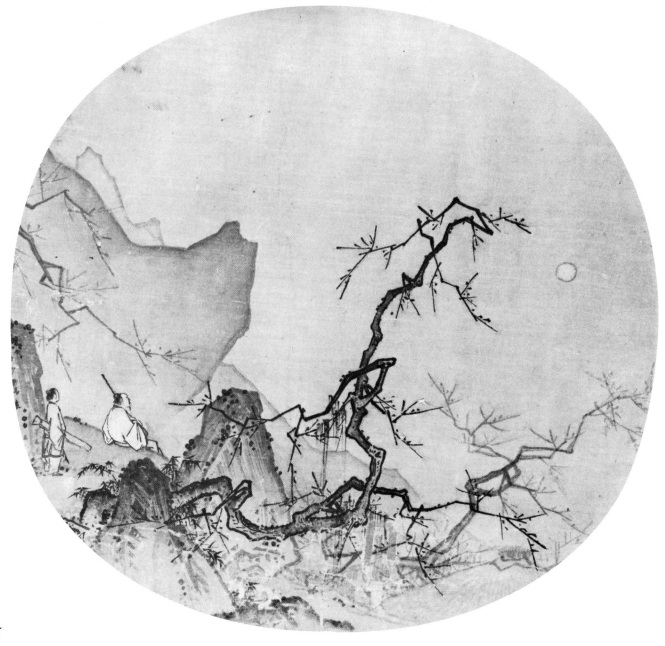

. . . a figure should seem to be contemplating the mountain;
the mountain, in turn, should seem to be bending over
and watching the figure. A lute player plucking his
instrument should appear also to be listening to the
moon, while the moon, calm and still, appears to be
listening to the notes of the lute.

Jie Zi Yuan Hua Zhuan

Written at Mauve Garden: Pine Wind Terrace

The mountain moon shines on a cloudless sky.
Deep in the night the wind rises among the pines.
I wish to weave my thoughts into a song for my jade lute,
But the pine wind never ceases blowing.

Zhu Yi-zun

*Ma Yuan (signed) (Late Twelfth to Thirteenth century): Fan-shaped album leaf,
ink and color on silk (10 1/8 x 10 1/2 inches). Courtesy of the collection of John M.
Crawford, Jr., New York.*

For Three Days I Traveled Through Mountains; When the Mountains Came to an End I Was Deeply Moved

Before my eyes, green mountains—
    I have truly loved them.
Why not have their craggy heights before me every day?
But this morning, the curtain fell,
    the mountains were swept away,
and I felt unhappy, as if I were saying goodbye
    to a friend.

                                        Yuan Zong-dao

The Autumn Is Beginning

Autumn is beginning, the weather is turning chill.
Crickets move in to sing under my bed.
A thousand things surge into my mind
And grieve my heart.
A thousand tales search for words;
But to whom will they be told?
The morning breeze flows under my sleeves,
The moonlight thins,
And the cock crows,
As I turn my horses' heads towards home.

                                        Ruan Ji

*Li Shan (Chin Dynasty): "Wind and Snow in the Fir-pines." Makimono
(12 5/16 x 395 inches). Handscroll. Courtesy of the Smithsonian Institution,
Freer Gallery of Art, Washington, D.C.*

Night

White night, the moon an unstrung bow,
The charred lampwick has half dozed off.
Mountain winds howl; deer unsettled;
Tree leaves drop; cicada alarmed.
For a while I remember delicacies east of the river,
And recall a boat under falling snow.
Barbarian songs arise, invading the very stars;
I'm empty, here at the edge of the sky.

Du Fu

Leaving Wang-Chuan Cottage

Sadly, with deep longing to stay on, I drive my
    carriage
Out of the pine trees twisted with vines . . .
I must endure the sorrow of leaving these
    green mountains,
But can I forget their blue streams?

Wang Wei

Shi Zhung (1437–1517): "Detail of Snow Landscape." Ink on silk (10 x 127 3/5 inches). Maria Antoinette Evans Fund 39.788. Courtesy, Museum of Fine Arts, Boston.

Selected Bibliography

Barnhart, Richard. *Wintry Forest, Old Trees.* New York: China Institute of America, 1972.

Binyon, Laurence. *The Flight of the Dragon.* New York: Grove Press, 1963.

———. *The Spirit of Man in Asian Art.* New York: Dover Publications, 1963.

Birch, Cyril, and Keene, Donald, eds. *Anthology of Chinese Literature.* New York: Grove Press, 1965.

Bynner, Witter, trans. *The Jade Mountain.* New York: Knopf, 1929.

Chang, Yin-nan and Walmsley, Lewis, trans. *Poems by Wang Wei.* Rutland, Vt.: Tuttle, 1958.

Chaves, Jonathan, trans. *Heaven My Blanket, Earth My Pillow: Poems by Yang Wan-Li.* New York: Weatherhill, 1975.

———, trans. *Pilgrim of the Clouds: Poems and Essays by Yüan Hung-tao and His Brothers.* New York: Weatherhill, 1978.

Ch'en, Jerome, and Bullock, Michael, trans. *Poems of Solitude.* New York: Abelard-Schuman, 1962.

Cooper, Arthur, trans. *Li Po and Tu Fu.* Baltimore: Penguin Books, 1973.

Davis, A. R., ed., Kotewall, Robert, and Smith, Norman L., trans. *The Penguin Book of Chinese Verse.* Baltimore: Penguin Books, 1962.

Fong, Wen. *Sung and Yüan Paintings.* New York: Metropolitan Museum of Art, 1973.

Grousset, René. *Chinese Art and Culture,* Chevalier, Haakon, trans. New York: Orion Press, 1959.

Lee, Sherman. *Chinese Landscape Painting.* The Cleveland Museum of Art, distributed by Prentice-Hall International, Inc. London.

Liu, James J. Y. *The Art of Chinese Poetry.* Chicago: University of Chicago Press, 1962.

Lo, Irving Yucheng, and Liu, Wu-chi, eds. *Sunflower Splendor: Three Thousand Years of Chinese Poetry.* Garden City, N.Y.: Anchor Books, Doubleday, 1975.

Payne, Robert, ed. *The White Pony: An Anthology of Chinese Poetry.* New York: New American Library, 1960.

Rexroth, Kenneth, trans. *100 Poems from the Chinese.* New York: New Directions, 1959.

Rowley, George. *Principals of Chinese Painting.* Princeton, N.J.: Princeton University Press, 1970.

Sakanishi, Shio, trans. *An Essay on Landscape Painting by Kuo Hsi*. London: John Murray, 1935.

———, trans. *The Spirit of the Brush*. London: John Murray, 1939.

Siren, Osvald. *The Chinese on the Art of Painting*. New York: Schocken Books, 1963.

Sze, Mai-mai, trans. and ed. *The Mustard Seed Garden Manual of Painting* by Chieh Tzu Yuan Hua Chuan. Princeton, N.J.: Princeton University Press, 1977.

Tagore, Amitendranath, trans. *Moments of Rising Mist: A Collection of Sung Landscape Poetry*. A Mushinsha Book, New York: Grossman Publishers, 1973.

Waley, Arthur, trans. *Chinese Poems*. London: Unwin Books, 1961.

———, trans. *A Hundred and Seventy Chinese Poems*. New York: Knopf, 1969.

Walmsley, Lewis and Dorothy. *Wang Wei, the Poet-Painter*. Rutland, Vt.: Tuttle, 1968.

Watson, Burton, trans. *Cold Mountain: 100 Poems by Han-shan*. New York: Grove Press, 1962.

Weng, Wan-go. *Chinese Painting and Calligraphy*. New York: Dover Publications, 1978.

Yee, Chian. *The Chinese Eye*. Bloomington: Indiana University Press, 1964.

Yip, Wai-lim, trans. *Hiding the Universe: Poems by Wang Wei*. A Mushinsha Book, New York: Grossman Publishers, 1972.

Index

Richard Lewis was born in New York City, where he now lives. After graduating from Bard College he embarked on a double career as teacher and author-editor. His early interest in the creative work of children led to his editing a variety of widely praised collections of writings by children—including *Miracles*, a collection of poetry by children from all over the world. He is also founder and director of the Touchstone Center—an interdisciplinary arts organization that works with both children and adults in schools and museums.

His interest in the Eastern perspective on life and nature has resulted in a number of books on Chinese and Japanese poetry and poets—among them *The Moment of Wonder*, *Of This World*, *The Way of Silence* and *In a Spring Garden*.